Read in 40 Hours or Less!

The Word's Greatest Secrets

Developed by R. L. Higgs

Published in the U.S.A

Printed in the United States of America

ISBN-13: 978-1981 884 926
ISBN-10: 1881 884 920

10 9 8 7 6 5 4 3 2 1

Layout and Cover Design by Linda Cline

Learning To Read Can Be Easy!

Learning to read is one of the most important tasks that a person can master. Without the alphabet, we can do very little. With the alphabet, however, we can do almost anything. The alphabet is a set of symbols representing the 44 sounds. Beginning with these sounds, and later, using essential interpretive skills, *Read in 40* prepares students to progress very quickly and naturally to the formation of words and the ability to decode the written and spoken word.

Mastery of the 44 sounds, the five *Read in 40* rules and the two decoding skills is the primary goal of this method. It is achieved by exercising patience, and by following the brief directions that precede each lesson. The student is placed on a 40 hour learning curve saturated with letters sounds and several thousands of drills. The reading skills are not mastered without effort, but in a few weeks they can be learned completely.

When a student or other individual learns that every letter in every word is in its place for a reason, that individual begins to understand the language better. The sounds and the skills involved in reading will meld very quickly, that individual will read, write, spell and speak Standard English confidently and fluently. Students will experience a definite change in attitude and behavior when, for the first time, they really see and know what reading is all about. They don't have to guess about many things anymore. They can read and understand.

Read in 40 was written purposefully with a broad range of people in mind. It teaches students of any age, culture, background and any ability, but it is especially useful for those grasping for help or who are convinced that they can't learn.

It is also important to remember that phonics cannot be isolated from other academics or areas of study. If you are studying science, math, history, computers, music, or any other subject, the language is all the same. ALL subjects work together under it.

Read in 40 is one of the most important of all learning experiences. It is essentially the key to all other learning, and through it, you will see improvement in all subject areas in a few short weeks. Just remember, learning to read can be easy.

What You Will Learn	Why
The Five Phonics Rules	The rules of phonics tell us when a vowel is long or short. Once mastered, reading is easy.
Blends, diphthongs, and digraphs	Blends help us hear and spell word patterns correctly.
Hard and soft C and G	These are two common letters that make more than one sound.
The two decoding skills for multisyllable words.	Decoding skills show how to read multi-syllable words.
When Y is a vowel	Sometimes Y is a consonant and sometimes it is a vowel and different rules apply.
Silent letter combinations and silent letters.	Silent letters are decoded in a special way.
Where to put the accent	Big words have accent rules.
This is a very straightforward phonics program. It is **not** a reading program. Phonics first, then reading is so easy!	The lessons are thoroughly explained. Students should show increased ability to analyze words, listen, express thoughts clearly, improve spelling, and apply skills to independent reading. Basically, that's all there is to it. Read the directions to your student when necessary.

Table of Contents

Learning To Read Can Be Easy! iii

Lesson 1:   **One Syllable Words** 1

Lesson 2:   **L Blends** 9

Lesson 3:   **R Blends** 13

Lesson 4:   **S Blends** 16

Lesson 5:   **The Three Letter Blends** 18

Lesson 6:   **R-Controlled Vowels** 23

Lesson 7:   **Diphthongs** 27

Lesson 8:   **Multi-Syllable Words** 33

Lesson 9:   **Adding ING** 41

Lesson 10:   **Consonant Digraphs** 45

Lesson 11:   **Vowel Digraphs** 51

Lesson 12:   **C and G** 56

Lesson 13:   **Y is a Vowel and a Consonant** 62

Lesson 14:   **Silent Letters** 65

Lesson 15:   **LE at the End of a Word** 67

Lesson 16:   **Syllabication** 68

Lesson 17   **The Big Words** 70

Ready Reference Guide 72

Lesson 1
One Syllable Words

Rule #1

When a vowel is followed by a consonant, the vowel is **short**.

The keyword is l ĭ p.

Rule #2

When a vowel is followed by two consonants, the vowel is **short**.

The keyword is h ă n d.

Rule #3

When a vowel is not followed by a consonant, the vowel is **long.**

The keyword is m ē.

Rule #4

When the last letter in a word is **e**, the **e** is silent and the first vowel is **long.**

The keyword is k ī t ҿ.

Rule #5

When vowels are next to each other, the first vowel is long and the second vowel is silent.

The keyword is r ē ҿ d.

Rule #1   When a vowel is followed by a consonant, the vowel is short.

The keyword is **lĭp**. To decode a one syllable word, look at the consonant that follows the vowel. In the word **lĭp**, the consonant that follows vowel i is **p**. Since **Rule #1** says that a vowel is short when it is followed by a consonant, and consonant **p** is to the right of vowel i, it must be the short vowel i.

Directions:
Say each word twice. Print the word in the space provided. Mark the vowel **short**.

1. man mă n	2. rub	3. bed
4. pig	5. mom	6. pop
7. ham	8. gag	9. had
10. bib	11. fib	12. did
13. cab	14. Ben	15. rot
16. ten	17. not	18. sun
19. jab	20. kit	21. tin
22. bug	23. bat	24. mid
25. lot	26. plug	27. slim
28. rug	29. let	30. lid
31. bun	32. bet	33. dot
34. hot	35. kin	36. get

Rule #2   When a vowel is followed by two consonants, the vowel is
             short.

The keyword is **hǎnd**. There are two consonants to the right of the vowel
a, they are **n** and **d**. Since the vowel **a** has two consonants after it, the
sound of the vowel **ǎ** is short as in **ǎt**.

Directions:
Say each word twice. Print the word in the space provided. Mark the
vowel **short**.

1. bent bĕnt	2. pond	3. bond
4. band	5. stamp	6. lump
7. sift	8. spend	9. bump
10. crisp	11. bunt	12. mist
13. trust	14. plant	15. cliff
16. nest	17. fond	18. blast
19. silk	20. wept	21. west

Rule #3   When a vowel is not followed by a consonant, the vowel is long.

The keyword is m **e.** Since the vowel **e** is not followed by a consonant, the sound of the vowel ē is long.

Directions:

Say each word twice. Print the word in the space provided. Mark the vowel **long** or **short** according to **Rules** **#1**, **#2**, or **#3**.

1. be bē	2. go	3. no
4. so	5. nest	6. me
7. we	8. camp	9. stop
10. run	11. brass	12. fluff
13. span	14. get	15. hint
16. will	17. beg	18. rent
19. drop	20. drum	21. bend

Rule #4   When the last letter in a one syllable word is e, it is silent
making the first vowel long.

Directions:

The keyword is **kīte̸**. Say each word twice. Print the word in the space
provided. Mark the vowel **long** and draw a line through silent **e**.

1. life līf e̸	2. rode	3. mule
4. flake	5. tube	6. hole
7. mine	8. dime	9. hive
10. flame	11. slope	12. mute
13. state	14. price	15. nine
16. cone	17. cute	18. bite
19. hide	20. face	21. cage
22. bake	23. tape	24. ice

Rule #5   When the vowels are next to each other, the first vowel is long and the second vowel is silent.

Directions:

The keyword is rēₐd. There are two vowels next to each other, ē and a. The first vowel e is long. The vowel next to it is a and it is silent. Always draw a line through the silent vowel.

Say each word twice. Print the word in the space provided. Mark the vowel **long** then draw a line through silent vowel.

1. read r ē ₐ d	2. suit	3. load
4. heat	5. coast	6. toe
7. green	8. tail	9. teen
10. brain	11. soap	12. sleep
13. road	14. leave	15. beam
16. mean	17. beat	18. creep
19. hoe	20. Joe	21. wait

Short Vowel Review

Directions:

Write each word in the space provided. Mark each vowel **long**, **short**, or **silent**.

1. mine	2. ditch	3. ice
4. cake	5. jump	6. bed
7. grace	8. tide	9. goat
10. met	11. meet	12. lot
13. use	14. Ed	15. ran
16. lead	17. deep	18. fade
19. made	20. fist	21. bone
22. meat	23. sheen	24. yank
25. cup	26. bean	27. joke
28. feast	29. maid	30. feet

Lesson 2
L Blends

There are two and three letter combinations that occur most often. These are called **blends** which are two or three letter consonants that stand together in many words. Each of the consonants keeps its own sound. Never separate them because they are treated as one unit. Blends can begin or end a word.

The blends are: bl   cl   fl   gl   pl   sl

Directions:

Say each word twice. Write the word in the box. Underline the blend.

bl	1. blast b̲l̲ă s t	2. bled	3. blot	4. blip	5. blue
cl	6. clap	7. clench	8. clot	9. clip	10. club
fl	11. flag	12. fled	13. flog	14. flip	15. flunk
gl	16. glad	17. glen	18. glob	19. glib	20. glum
pl	21. plan	22. pled	23. plot	24. pliers	25. plum
sl	26. slap	27. sled	28. slot	29. slid	30. slum

L Blends

Directions:

Write the word in the box. Underline the blend. Decode each word.

Remember blends are treated as one sound

1. blot b l ŏ t	2. club	3. flag
4. flip	5. glen	6. plug
7. plop	8. plum	9. plan
10. slit	11. flop	12. clip
13. fled	14. flub	15. clam
16. flip	17. flat	18. glum
19. flock	20. flick	21. fleece

More L Blends

Directions:

Write the word in the box. Underline the blend. Decode each word.

1. sled	2. glib	3. plan
4. plant	5. plot	6. bless
7. club	8. flavor	9. bleach
10. glad	11. flag	12. float
13. black	14. blame	15. plate
16. blend	17. peak	18. slam
19. sled	20. fleet	21. slam

Blends Review

Directions:

Decode each word by underlining each blend, and mark each vowel short, long, or silent.

1. plead	2. black	3. plus
4. slope	5. plum	6. plank
7. plain	8. slug	9. slash
10. slack	11. slim	12. slime
13. slip	14. slam	15. sleeve
16. slang	17. slice	18. flesh
19. clutch	20. glib	21. glee
22. globe	23. plan	24. glass
25. blunt	26. please	27. blush
28. clip	29. clan	30. clamp

Lesson 3

R Blends

The R blends are: br   cr   dr   fr   gr   pr   tr

Directions:

Write the word in the box. Underline the blends. Mark each vowel as long, short, or silent. Then, read all of the words aloud.

br	1. bran b r ă n	2. breed	3. broke	4. brim	5. brush
cr	6. crab	7. crept	8. crop	9. crib	10. crumb
dr	11. drag	12. dream	13. drop	14. drip	15. drum
fr	16. frame	17. freed	18. frog	19. frill	20. fruit
gr	21. grand	22. greet	23. groan	24. grill	25. grub
pr	26. prank	27. press	28. prod	29. prim	30. prune
tr	31. trap	32. trek	33. trod	34. trip	35. true

R Blends

Directions:

Write the word in the box. Decode, read aloud, and write each word.

1. trot trŏt	2. grub	3. drip
4. cram	5. prim	6. brag
7. trim	8. fret	9. prod
10. brick	11. drum	12. drag
13. crab	14. brat	15. brush
16. craze	17. crash	18. creep
19. crest	20. crease	21. crave

R Blends Review

Directions:

Write the word in the box. Decode, read aloud, write, and decode each word.

1. Brad	2. cramp	3. drag
4. drum	5. Fred	6. prop
7. brain	8. brake	9. dread
10. brim	11. draft	12. drift
13. crest	14. creak	15. creep
16. cross	17. crop	18. kite
19. crust	20. dram	21. crumb
22. drone	23. drive	24. drap
25. green	26. dress	27. prize
28. trap	29. bran	30. drop

Lesson 4

S Blends

The S blends are: sc   sk   sm   sn   sp   st   sw

Directions:

Write the word in the box. Underline the blends. Mark each vowel as long or short. Read all of the words aloud.

sc	1. scat s c ă t	2. screen	3. scope	4. script	5. scum
sk	6. skate	7. sketch	8. skin	9. skip	10. skull
sm	11. small	12. smell	13. smoke	14. smite	15. smug
sn	16. snap	17. sneeze	18. snipe	19. snide	20. snub
sp	21. space	22. spell	23. spot	24. spin	25. spurt
st	26. stamp	27. step	28. stop	29. stir	30. stump
sw	31. swam	32. swell	33. swing	34. swipe	35. swum

S Blends Review

Directions:

Write the word in the box. Underline the blends. Mark each vowel long, short or silent. Then, read all of the words aloud.

1. stage s̲t̲āg̶e̶	2. snake	3. skull
4. stung	5. snob	6. space
7. steep	8. steal	9. still
10. small	11. snail	12. waist
13. feast	14. least	15. pest
16. swell	17. sweet	18. snip
19. stop	20. stiff	21. street
22. snub	23. spine	24. skip
25. skate	26. speak	27. smoke
28. snack	29. spell	30. smell

Lesson 5

The Three Letter Blends

The three letter blends are: scr   spr   str   spl   squ

Directions:

Practice marking the vowels long or short and reading these words with three letter blends. Write the word in the box provided. Underline the blends.

1. scrub s c r ŭ b	2. strip	3. split	4. squid
5. stress	6. scream	7. scrap	8. street
9. stride	10. scrimp	11. stress	12. strove
13. strive	14. stroke	15. strike	16. squeeze
17. scram	18. strain	19. stray	20. strap
21. spray	22. screen	23. sprite	24. stock
25. splice	26. stop	27. squat	28. spread
29. squint	30. squat	31. scroll	32. scribe

Remember the *Read in 40* Rules

1. If a vowel has one consonant, it is **short**.
2. If a vowel has two consonants, it is **short**.
3. If a vowel has no consonant, it is **long**.
4. When e is at the end of a word, it is **silent** and the first vowel is **long**.
5. When two vowels are next to each other, the first is **long** and the second is **silent**.

Directions:

Decode both words. See what a difference a vowel can make!

1. am → aim ăm → āi̶m	2. red → read rĕd → rēa̶d	3. mad → maid
4. bed → bead	5. pad → paid	6. met → meet
7. bat → bait	8. fed → feed	9. lad → laid
10. led → lead	11. Brad → braid	12. step → steep
13. net → neat	14. bled → bleed	15. cost → coast
16. men → mean	17. plan → plain	18. clam → claim
19. pal → pail	20. bran → brain	21. pet → peat
22. man → main	23. did → died	24. pant → paint

Review

More Vowels to Figure Out – Long or Silent?

Directions:

Are these vowels long, short, or silent? Decode and remember to cross out the silent vowels.

1. rain	2. mail	3. coal	4. pain
5. bean	6. loaf	7. team	8. oak
9. feet	10. lean	11. feed	12. cue
13. seal	14. bean	15. deep	16. feel
17. mine	18. deal	19. seed	20. foam
21. coach	22. weak	23. week	24. sheep
25. sea	26. see	27. main	28. meat
29. loan	30. free	31. moat	32. toast

Mixed Review

Directions:

Decode and remember to cross out the silent vowels.

1. pleat	2. plead	3. stain	4. speed
5. gleam	6. loan	7. greed	8. saint
9. suit	10. wait	11. seat	12. dried
13. strip	14. need	15. show	16. chick
17. brag	18. glass	19. pain	20. blast
21. drum	22. fruit	23. dream	24. trap
25. smug	26. stir	27. stud	28. week
29. small	30. trot	31. drain	32. cram

Mixed Review

Directions:

Decode.

1. braid	2. steel	3. skin	4. skill
5. wind	6. wine	7. beef	8. steal
9. sprain	10. greet	11. plain	12. grain
13. east	14. stream	15. crave	16. cream
17. peep	18. steam	19. wheat	20. cheek
21. treat	22. free	23. bleed	24. float
25. strain	26. claim	27. tree	28. drift
29. meet	30. keen	31. smell	32. skip
33. laid	34. seen	35. chin	36. steal

Lesson 6

R-Controlled Vowels

This family of sounds includes words made from a vowel and consonant **r**. When decoding do not separate them. They are as one. When decoding, <u>underline</u> them.

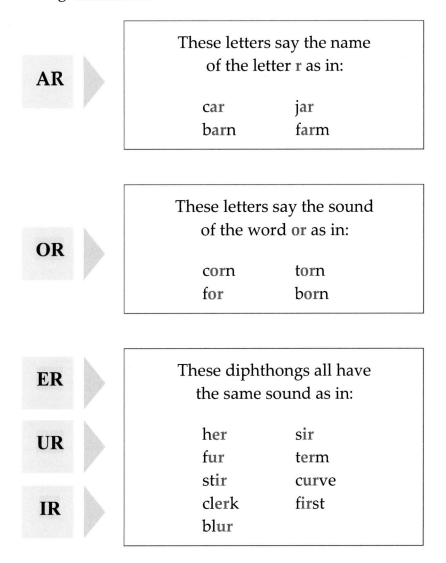

AR → These letters say the name of the letter **r** as in:

car	jar
barn	farm

OR → These letters say the sound of the word **or** as in:

corn	torn
for	born

ER
UR
IR → These diphthongs all have the same sound as in:

her	sir
fur	term
stir	curve
clerk	first
blur	

R-Controlled Vowels

Directions:

Arm has the sound **ar** stands for. Decode the words below and underline the **ar** diphthongs and blends. However, mark all vowels long, short, or silent using the five phonics rules.

1. arm a r m	2. cart	3. mark
4. star	5. mart	6. barn
7. shark	8. art	9. tar
10. car	11. yarn	12. dart
13. yard	14. far	15. harp
16. dark	17. carve	18. arch
19. garb	20. harm	21. bark
22. darn	23. spark	24. park
25. march	26. sharp	27. charm

R-Controlled Vowels

Directions:

ER, **IR**, and **UR** all share the same sound. Write the word in each box and decode.

1. her	2. fern	3. berth
4. skirt	5. girl	6. burst
7. third	8. firm	9. shirt
10. squirrel	11. fir	12. fur
13. squirt	14. bird	15. flirt
16. dirt	17. cert	18. Burt
19. purr	20. curve	21. purse

R-Controlled Vowels Mixed Review

Directions:

Decode and write all of the words.

1. jerk	2. burn
3. pork	4. fork
5. perk	6. target
7. hurt	8. sleek
9. cloak	10. beak
11. sir	12. third
13. smile	14. learn
15. term	16. cord
17. twirl	18. short
19. start	20. church
21. chore	22. curve
23. dirt	24. spark
25. germ	26. skirt
27. purse	28. target
29. nurse	30. bore

Lesson 7
Diphthongs

This family of sounds includes diphthongs made from a combination of vowels and special letters.

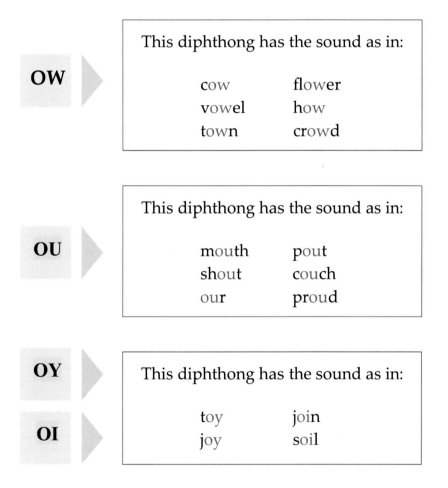

OW

This diphthong has the sound as in:

cow	flower
vowel	how
town	crowd

OU

This diphthong has the sound as in:

mouth	pout
shout	couch
our	proud

OY

OI

This diphthong has the sound as in:

toy	join
joy	soil

Diphthongs

Treat a diphthong as one vowel sound. Fortunately, they always keep the same sounds. They are neither long nor short. They say the same sound every time so this will not be difficult to master.

Directions:

The diphthong <u>ow</u> and <u>ou</u> have the same sound. Print the word in the box.

<u>Underline</u> the diphthongs.

1. cow	2. out	3. vowel
4. bout	5. found	6. house
7. round	8. clown	9. couch
10. pound	11. pout	12. now
13. proud	14. pound	15. foul
16. shower	17. cloud	18. towel
19. scowl	20. flower	21. sprout

Diphthong <u>ow</u> and Vowel Sound ōw

Directions:

The diphthong <u>ow</u> and <u>ou</u> have the same sound. Print the word in the box. <u>Underline</u> the diphthongs.

1. tow	2. how	3. grow	4. bowl
5. now	6. vowel	7. town	8. yellow
9. flower	10. clown	11. shower	12. throw
13. show	14. slow	15. howl	16. flow

ōw the vowel sound	<u>ow</u> the diphthong
1.　　tōw	2.　　h <u>o w</u>
3.	4.
5.	6.
7.	8.
9.	10.
11.	12.
13.	14.
15.	16.

Diphthongs oy, oi

Directions:

The diphthong **oy** as in **boy**, and the diphthong **oi** as in **oil**, have the same sound. <u>Underline</u> each diphthong.

1. spoil sp<u>oi</u>l	2. oil	3. toy
4. broil	5. choice	6. coin
7. coy	8. boy	9. foil
10. noise	11. coil	12. join
13. Roy	14. soil	15. moist
16. boil	17. joy	18. point

Diphthong <u>ew</u>

Directions:

Blew has the sound that the diphthong **ew** stands for. Say each word twice. Choose the answer from the list below. Write the answer in the box at the right.

chew	mew	stew
flew	few	news
screwdriver		

A. What must you do to your food before you swallow it?	
B. What is a tool?	
C. How did birds travel to the south?	
D. What is the sound made by a cat?	
E. If you didn't have many coins, how many would you have?	
F. What may be good or bad? You hear about it in many ways.	
G. What can you eat?	

Diphthongs

Directions:

Say each word twice. Underline the diphthongs **oy, oi, ew.**

1. blew	2. grew	3. dew
4. screw	5. slew	6. threw
7. new	8. pew	9. mew
10. few	11. blew	12. moist
13. new	14. chew	15. spoil
16. drew	17. noise	18. soil
19. pew	20. flew	21. drew
22. chew	23. brew	24. crew
25. news	26. stew	27. choice
28. coil	29. broil	30. toy

Lesson 8

Multi-Syllable Words

Ten Steps to Reading Fluently

So far you have learned how to decode one-syllable words by applying the rules of phonics. They helped you figure out if a vowel is long, short or silent. In this lesson you will learn how to divide a word into syllables. Once a word is divided into syllables you will apply the phonics rules which will enable you to read just about everything! From hereafter you will be able to read multi-syllable words with three, four and more syllables – the really big words in 40 hours or less!

To read words with more than one syllable

1. Divide the word into single syllables.
2. Apply the rules for single syllables.
3. Determine if the vowel is long, short or silent.

Decoding rules tell us **where** to divide a word into syllables. Phonics tells us if a **consonant** is a blend, and if a **vowel** is long, short, or silent. If you have followed the directions for each lesson so far, you have already decoded more than 1,000 words. Yeah!

10 Steps to Reading *BIG* Words Fluently

1   Begin by only looking at the first letter of the word, then the second, third and so forth. Only look at the whole word. Do nothing.

2   Now go back to the first vowel. Talk to it. Ask it if it has one or two consonants to its immediate right. Divide the vowel according to the two decoding rules.

3   Draw a box around the first syllable.

4   In the first box, mark the vowel long, short or silent according to the phonics rules. The first syllable is done.

5   Go to the second vowel. Talk to the second vowel. Ask it if it has one or two consonants to its immediate right, then divide the vowel as usual according to the two decoding rules.

6   Draw a box around the second syllable. Repeat steps one through five. If there are three vowel sounds in a word, then there are three syllables in that word, and you will have to draw three boxes. If there are five vowel sounds, then there are five syllables in that word, and you will have to draw five boxes, etc.

7   Pronounce clearly every letter and every sound in the first box, the second box and every box.

8   Only read one syllable at a time. You know the vowels so you don't have to guess anymore. You already know the consonant sounds because they keep their same sounds.

9   Decode every word in this book, then say it three times. Why say the words out loud? Because the fast path to learning anything is from:

your mouth ⇨ to your ears ⇨ into your brain

10   Practice. Practice. Practice

Everyone who reads well decodes. They just do it very, very fast, almost automatically without thinking about it. With practice so will you. I promise. This is easy.

NOTE: There are exceptions to all rules. There are even exceptions to our decoding rules which we will discuss latter.

Decoding Skill #1

When a vowel is followed by one consonant, separate the vowel from the consonant.

STEP 1   When a vowel is followed by one consonant, split them up and box it. Vowel **o** has one consonant after it, **t**.

> | h o | t e l

STEP 2   Look at Step 1 above. Vowel **o** is marked long because the phonics rule says: *When a vowel stands alone, it is long.* The first syllable is **hō**.

> | h ō | t e l

STEP 3   Draw a box around **t e l**, the last syllable, and the last vowel.

> | h ō | | t e l |

STEP 4   Look at Step 3 above. Vowel **e** has one consonant *l*. It is short because the phonics rule says: *If a vowel has one consonant, then it is short.* The last syllable is **tĕl**.

> | h ō | | t ĕ l |

The word is: **ho + tel**

Decoding Skill #1

Blends, diphthongs, and digraphs are one unit. Underline them. They are joined, married, and must stay together. Another set of blends are the double **LL** blends:

all   ell   ill   oll   ull

Directions:

Decode. You may use a slash from now on instead of a box to separate syllables.

1. motel mō / tĕl	2. bacon
3. silent	4. rodent
5. spider	6. recap
7. grocer	8. pupil
9. stable	10. diner
11. taken	12. lady
13. defend	14. recent
15. prevent	16. vacant

Decoding Skill #1

1. precept	2. human
3. even	4. Polish
5. clover	6. robust
7. emit	8. rebel
9. crisis	10. cement
11. stolen	12. rival
13. locust	14. minus
15. raven	16. negate
17. tulip	18. diet

Decoding Skill #2

STEP 1 When a vowel has two consonants split them up and box it. Consonants t and t are split up. First decode the first syllable.

STEP 2 Look at Step 1 above. Vowel **u** is marked short because the phonics rule says: *When a vowel is followed by a consonant, it is short*. The first syllable is

STEP 3 Draw a box around t o n, the last syllable.

STEP 4 Look at Step 3 above. Vowel **o** has one consonant **n**. Vowel **o** is

The word is: **but + ton**

Directions:

Decode the words below. Remember, when a vowel is followed by two consonants, split them up.

1. campus căm/pŭs	2. pigment
3. compute	4. cinder
5. jumbo	6. blunder
7. indent	8. except
9. number	10. member
11. dandruff	12. lobster
13. concrete	14. summit
15. import	16. decode
17. button	18. slender
19. canvas	20. content

Decoding Skills – Mixed Review

1. prorate	2. polite
3. embrace	4. microbe
5. biology	6. delete
7. advance	8. elementary
9. athlete	10. humane
11. console	12. calibrate
13. brocade	14. profane
15. combine	16. decline
17. prudent	18. breve
19. crusade	20. insinuate
21. instigate	22. insulate
23. modem	24. manufacture
25. cumulate	26. magnetize

Lesson 9
Adding ING

When a vowel is followed by one consonant, the vowel is short. Just add another consonant plus i n g.

Rule #1   When a vowel is followed by one consonant, the vowel is short. Just add another consonant plus ing.

nod + d + ing = nodding

Rule #2   When a vowel is followed by two consonants, the vowel is short. Just add ing.

hunt + ing = hunting

Rule #3   When a vowel stands alone, it is long. Simply add ing.

gō + ing = gōing

Rule #4   Silent e makes the first vowel long. First drop the silent e, then add ing.

rāve + ing = rāving

Rule #5   With adjacent vowels, the first vowel is long and the second vowel is silent.

bōat + ing = bōating

Directions:

Rewrite the words adding **ing**. Apply Rules 1 or 2.

1. slip *slipping*	2. yell	3. stop
4. fuss	5. bet	6. mend
7. bump	8. clot	9. fit
10. will	11. tell	12. spin
13. drop	14. rent	15. log
16. send	17. jog	18. hunt
19. bat	20. hit	21. scat
22. strip	23. limp	24. turn
25. miss	26. help	27. top
28. hint	29. call	30. cut

Directions:

Rewrite the words adding ing. Apply Rules 3 or 4

1. go *going*	2. be	3. note
4. take	5. name	6. smile
7. poke	8. paste	9. hope
10. dive	11. drive	12. rave
13. rope	14. time	15. write
16. ride	17. tame	18. blame
19. bake	20. rake	21. cake
22. paste	23. blaze	24. tame
25. smoke	26. vote	27. state
28. frame	29. save	30. joke

Directions:

Apply Rule 5 when adding **ing** which says: *With adjacent vowels, just add* **ing**.

1. meet *meeting*	2. keep	3. boat
4. nail	5. eat	6. plead
7. clean	8. moan	9. soak
10. soap	11. sleep	12. leap
13. coast	14. leak	15. load
16. foam	17. boast	18. coat
19. loan	20. float	21. tail
22. sail	23. toast	24. wait
25. loaf	26. rain	27. boast
28. roam	29. fail	30. sail

Lesson 10

Consonant Digraphs

Digraphs are made up of 2 letters even though they have only one sound. They are considered one unit and cannot be separated. Consonant digraphs can come at the beginning or end of a word. Never mark digraphs long or short. Underline digraphs.

th   as in thumb

wh as in wheel

sh   as in shoe

ch   as in church

Consonant Digraphs Hard and Soft TH

The **th** in *thorn* and *bath* have the soft sound of **th**. While the **th** in *that* and *bathe* have the hard sound of **th**.

Directions:

Say each word twice then underline the **th**.

1. thumb	2. thin	3. them
4. mother	5. the	6. fifth
7. those	8. father	9. thank
10. that	11. cloth	12. filth
13. teeth	14. then	15. them
16. path	17. with	18. fiftieth
19. then	20. bath	21. bathe
22. think	23. these	24. this
25. three	26. moth	27. fortieth
28. ruthless	29. thick	30. third

Consonant Digraph WH

Wheel begins the sound that **wh** stands for.

Directions:

Say the word twice then underline the **wh**.

1. wheel	2. whom	3. whale
4. white	5. whiff	6. wholesale
7. wharf	8. whammy	9. whole
10. whittle	11. whorl	12. whirl
13. whimpering	14. whip	15. whisk
16. whiff	17. where	18. which
19. who	20. what	21. whoa
22. whither	23. whopper	24. white
25. whist	26. whig	27. whiskers
28. whistle	29. wheat	30. whisper

Consonant Digraph SH

Shell begins with the sound representing **sh**

Directions:

Say each word twice then underline the **sh**.

1. ship	2. shade	3. shell
4. blush	5. thrush	6. wishbone
7. shaker	8. shoe	9. short
10. trash	11. rash	12. cash
13. shirt	14. sheep	15. shallow
16. shall	17. fishbone	18. brush
19. dash	20. shaft	21. shore
22. shack	23. shoulder	24. shake
25. shrimp	26. shopping	27. sheet
28. shadow	29. shelf	30. dish

Consonant Digraph CH

Chair begins with the sound representing **ch**.

Directions:

Say each word twice then underline the **ch**.

1. chill	2. child	3. match
4. catch	5. chili	6. crutch
7. leach	8. chump	9. cheese
10. checks	11. hitch	12. witch
13. peach	14. chimney	15. chipmunk
16. chip	17. chicks	18. chat
19. cherry	20. chain	21. chamber
22. check	23. patch	24. latch
25. pitch	26. chopsticks	27. chore
28. chilly	29. checkers	30. chimp

Consonant Digraph Review

Directions:

Say each word twice. Listen for a beginning, middle, or ending consonant digraph sound. Decode each word in the space provided.

1. shade	2. whale	3. shell
4. peach	5. wishbone	6. thatch
7. church	8. chair	9. whiskers
10. while	11. with	12. branch
13. shear	14. shallow	15. beach
16. ranch	17. blush	18. shrimp
19. whistle	20. fortieth	21. three
22. whisker	23. shovel	24. path
25. bath	26. short	27. chimp
28. checks	29. which	30. moth

Lesson 11

Vowel Digraphs

Digraphs are made up of two letters even though they have only one sound. They are considered one unit and cannot be separated. Vowel digraphs are counted as one syllable. Never mark digraphs long or short. Underline digraphs.

oo as in zoo

ea as in bread

oo as in book

au as in auto

Vowel Digraph oo

The vowel digraph **oo** has two sounds: **oo** as in zoo, and **oo** as in book.

Directions:

Read each word out loud.

1. zoo	2. tooth	3. broom
4. hood	5. moot	6. too
7. moo	8. zoom	9. booth
10. spool	11. pool	12. hoof
13. root	14. roof	15. noon
16. boot	17. tool	18. soon
19. spoon	20. hoof	21. good
22. coon	23. boo	24. mood
25. rooster	26. wood	27. cooler
28. coop	29. cookie	30. loose

Vowel Digraphs au, aw

The vowel digraph **au** as in laundry and the vowel **aw** as in saw stand for the same sound.

Directions:

Underline the **au** and **aw**.

1. paw	2. aunt	3. mauve
4. awful	5. awning	6. yawn
7. causal	8. saucepan	9. dawn
10. claw	11. sauna	12. auto
13. saw	14. taught	15. because
16. raw	17. fawn	18. pawn
19. audio	20. Caucasian	21. August
22. hawk	23. draw	24. awe
25. saucer	26. pause	27. crawl

Vowel Digraph – Mixed Practice

Bread has a sound that the vowel digraph **ea** stands for.

Directions:

Say each word twice. Below <u>underline</u> the digraph <u>ea</u> in each word.

1. bread	2. leather	3. feather
4. sweater	5. breakfast	6. breath
7. thread	8. weather	9. break
10. stead	11. deaf	12. wealth

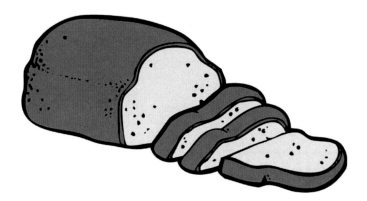

Review

Directions:

Say each word twice, then decode as usual.

1. lead	2. saw	3. mausoleum
4. saucer	5. breath	6. authentic
7. hauled	8. fawn	9. aurora
10. tray	11. caucus	12. pause
13. law	14. raw	15. wheat
16. moon	17. spoon	18. auto
19. break	20. hawk	21. sauce
22. awning	23. shadow	24. zoo
25. peach	26. tooth	27. thistle
28. shrimp	29. chocolate	30. loot

Lesson 12

C and G

You will learn:

- To read with the hard and soft sounds of c and g
- That a hard c and hard g are usually followed by vowels a, o, or u
- That a soft c and soft g are usually followed by e, i, or y
- That soft c sounds like s and hard c sounds like k
- That soft g sounds like j and hard g sounds like g

1. can _____   5. con _____
2. cat _____   6. cap _____
3. cram _____   7. cord _____
4. cub _____   8. custom _____

1. glad _____   5. gage _____
2. gore _____   6. get _____
3. go _____   7. gray _____
4. got _____   8. game _____

Soft C

Which vowels follow soft c?

Directions:

Put s under soft c words and decode.

1. cedar sēdar	2. cell	3. cent	4. prince
5. race	6. glance	7. cease	8. city
9. cinch	10. circus	11. citrus	12. dance

Hard C

Which vowels follow hard c?

Directions

Put a k under hard c words, and decode.

1. can kăn	2. cut	3. come	4. correct
5. comet	6. cub	7. curl	8. cure
9. coma	10. care	11. cash	12. car

Soft G

Directions:

Put a j under the soft g words and decode.

1. gem j ĕ m	2. gene	3. germ	4. wage
5. giant	6. gym	7. age	8. gent
9. stage	10. page	11. plunge	12. cage

Hard G

Which vowels follow hard **g**?

Directions:

Decode hard **g** words as usual.

1. go 　 g ō	2. gab	3. game	4. garden
5. gas	6. gold	7. good	8. gum
9. gate	10. got	11. frog	12. gaze

Review Lessons 1 through 12

☐ Print the alphabet in lower and upper case.

☐ Print and say the names of each consonant.

☐ Print and say the names of each short vowel.

☐ Print and say the names of each long vowel.

☐ Print and say the Phonics Rules for one syllable words; give an example of each.

☐ Print and say the l blends; r blends; s blends; give examples of each.

☐ Print and say the vowel digraphs and consonant digraphs; give examples of each.

☐ Print and say the diphthongs; give an example of each.

☐ Give two examples of hard c and hard g.

☐ Give two examples of soft c and soft g.

Congratulations! If you have answered
most of the review questions correctly, you
have mastered the sounds of English.

Lesson 13

Y is a Vowel and a Consonant

When is Y a Consonant?
If Y starts a word, it is a consonant.

yes   yard   yell   yank   yam

When is Y a Vowel?
if y is inside a one syllable word,
y has the sound of long or short vowel i.

myth = mĭth   syrup = sĭrŭp
style = stīle   type = tīpͯ

Another Y if y is at the end of a word,
y has the sound of long vowel e.

play = plāͯ   baby = bābē

Just One More Y
if y is the only vowel,
it sounds like long ī

my = mī   by = bī   try = trī

Directions:

Decode the following words.

1. Lynn Lĭnn	2. crypt
3. style	4. by
5. cry	6. try
7. spy	8. yes
9. yell	10. yard
11. yank	12. type
13. story	14. sky
15. play	16. thyme
17. day	18. key
19. stray	20. gray
21. clay	22. fly
23. pyle	24. sty
25. cyd	26. cyst

To add **s** or **ed** to a word that ends in **y**, just change the **y** to an **i**.

Directions:

Change **y** to an **i** then add either **ed** or **es** to the end of the word.

	Add es	Add ed
1. reply r e p l ī	replies	replied
2. copy		
3. study		
4. multiply		
5. balcony		
6. cavity		
7. apology		
8. country		
9. society		
10. steady		
11. classify		
12. notify		

Lesson 14
Silent Letters

Prepare to Learn:
1. How to read words with silent letter combinations.
2. To recognize when consonants are silent.
3. To read eight silent consonant combinations:

       gn   kn   mb   lm   wh   sw   wr   pb

- Whenever **gn** starts a word, the **g** is silent. Draw a line through g.

    g̶ n a t   g̶ n a s h   g̶ n a w

- Whenever **kn** starts a word the **k** is silent. Draw a line through k.

    K̶ n o t   K̶ n i t   K̶ n o b

- Whenever **wr** starts a word the **w** is silent. Draw a line through w.

    w̶ r e c k   w̶ r a t h   w̶ r-a n g l e

- Whenever **wh** starts a word the **h** is silent. Draw a line through h.

    w h̶ e e z e   w h̶ a l e   w h̶ e r e

- Sometimes when the **sw** combination is in a word, the **w** is silent.

    s w̶ o r d   a n s w̶ e r

- Sometimes when the **lm** combination is in a word, the **l** is silent.

    p a l̶ m   a l̶ m o n d s

- Sometimes when the **pb** combination is in a word, the **p** is silent.

    c u p̶ b o a r d   r a s p̶ b e r r y

- Whenever the **mb** combination is at the end of a word, the **b** is silent.

    l i m b̶ s   c r u m b̶ s

Silent Letter Review

Directions:

Cross off silent letters.

1. knot K̶nŏt	2. knit	3. knife
4. know	5. knob	6. knew
7. wrong	8. kneel	9. knapsack
10. knees	11. knuckles	12. knockout
13. write	14. wreck	15. wrap
16. wreath	17. wrist	18. wren
19. wrench	20. typewriter	21. wrapper
22. twitch	23. wrong	24. wrack
25. wrung	26. wrestle	27. wrinkle
28. whine	29. whirl	30. whim

Lesson 15

LE at the End of a Word

How to decode the word: table ⇨ tā / ble
    but it sounds like ⇨ tā / bul

How to decode the word: staple ⇨ stā / ple
    but it sounds like ⇨ stā / pul

Some words ending in **le** are:

maple	purple	fable	marble	giggle	cable
scramble	noble	able	idle	turtle	apple
buckle	people	needle	table	bubbles	kettle
ramble	candle	rattle	eagle	sprinkle	

Can you think of some more words ending in **le**?

1. _____

2. _____

3. _____

4. _____

5. _____

6. _____

7. _____

8. _____

9. _____

10. _____

Lesson 16

Syllabication

There are exceptions to the phonics rules. Sometimes when we decode not all the words decode perfectly, though most of them do. That leaves us with that pesky few that do not decode perfectly. For example, camel. If we follow the decoding rules then camel could decode **cā/měl**. The long **ā** is wrong.

Here is what you must do. **If the vowel decodes long and wrong, change it to a short vowel!** After all, if a vowel is not long, then it usually is short. Isn't that simple?

If the word is…	and you decode to…	then change it to…
1. river	rī / ver	rĭv / er
2. proper		
3. credit		
4. liver		

If the vowel decodes short and wrong, change it to a long vowel.

5. most		
6. host		
7. kind		
8. child		

GH Has Three Sounds

1. **gh** can be silent as in:

   sigh   tigh   bright   sight   night

2. **gh** can sound like **f** as in:

   rough   tough   enough   cough

3. **gh** can sound like **g** as in:

   ghost   ghetto   ghastly

Lesson 17

The Big Words

The following word list is to help you build a more educated vocabulary. By now you should be very capable. You can decode all of the words even though you do not yet know them.

These lists have been edited by an experienced staff who believe it will serve well those who want a handy list of vocabulary words. Even though some of the words are from foreign languages, they are all subject to *Read in 40* rules.

Nonetheless, you may be wondering **why do I need such an extensive vocabulary?** When that question was put to a group of *Read in 40* parents and students they responded with the following remarks:

a. To have a more educated vocabulary for my kids.

b. To be able to discuss politics and social issues.

c. To write better letters.

d. To make posters for church.

e. So people won't talk over my head.

f. To read and write stories.

g. To read and write charts and maps.

h. To better understand newspapers and magazines.

i. To know what they are really talking about on the evening news.

j. To read better.

Perhaps one of the best reasons to study words is what a 5th grade boy said:
"I just want to know that I know – just in case I ever need to know."

Whatever your reason – it's a good thing. Go ahead – give the list a try – simply do your best, and ENJOY!

GOOD READING!

Directions:

Decode each word and use in a sentence.

1. bifurcate	26. perlocution
2. abdicate	27. attenuate
3. simultaneous	28. sycophant
4. perseverance	29. intrepid
5. indelible	30. shambolic
6. inalienable	31. surly
7. dissipate	32. obfuscate
8. condescend	33. rove
9. cessation	34. rocent
10. anesthetic	35. encomium
11. compliant	36. plutocrat
12. eligible	37. apoplectic
13. copious	38. arete
14. collateral	39. pugilist
15. enigma	40. salubrious
16. conscience	41. arcadian
17. exception	42. ludicrous
18. olfactory	43. anthropocentric
19. consensus	44. pontificate
20. colloquial	45. pernicious
21. confidential	46. precipitate
22. equipped	47. maven
23. altruistic	48. pangram
24. loquacious	49. lugubrious
25. inveigle	50. alienist

Ready Reference Guide

Consonants: B C D F G H J K L M N P Q R S T V W X Y Z
C and K share a sound. Q has no sound. V never stands alone
at the end of a word, an E always stands with it.

Vowel Sound	Key Word		Vowel Sound	Key Word
short a	at		el	well
short e	Ed		ol	old
short i	itch		ul	bull
short o	octopus		il	will
short u	up		au	Paul
long a	able		aw	saw
long e	easy		ou	out
long i	ice		ow	cow
long o	open		oi	oil
long u	use		oy	boy
ar	are		oo	zoo
er	her		oo	book
or	or		y	toy
ir	sir		aw	claw
ur	purr		au	auto
al	ball		ea	head

Apply Phonics Rules for Vowels

1. pĕt   When a vowel is followed by a consonant the vowel is **short**.
2. hūnt   When a vowel is followed by two consonants the vowel is **short**.
3. mē   When a vowel stands alone it is **long**.
4. līkҳ   Silent e makes the first vowel **long**.
5. bō̄ҳt   When vowels are adjacent, the first vowel is **long**, the second is **silent**.

Type 1 syllable:

When a vowel is followed by one consonant, split them up, then apply the phonetic rules to each syllable, one at time. (vowel/consonant) (vowel consonant/consonant)

l ā /d y   d ē /f ĕ n d   g r ō /c e r

Type 2 syllable:

When a vowel is followed by two consonants, split them up, then apply the phonetic rules to each syllable one at a time.

n ă p /k ĭ n   d ĭ n /n e r   l ŏ b /s t e r

Made in the USA
Monee, IL
13 January 2023

24021979R00048